Shopkeeper

Margaret Hudson

Contents

Where in the world?

Every day people visit shops to buy the things they need. The shops we visit most are the ones that sell us food. All over the world there are different people who run food shops.

We are going to visit four of these people.

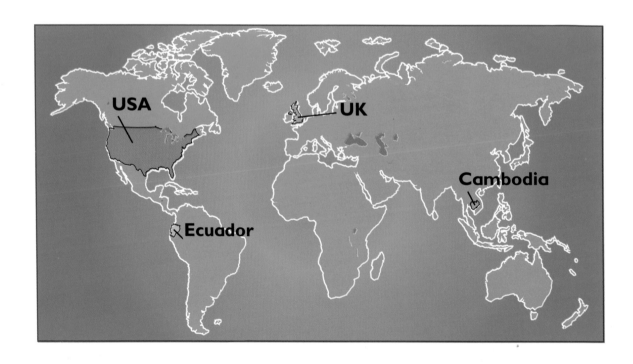

Bob and his wife run a **supermarket** in Des Moines, Iowa, in the United States of America (USA).

Sovon and her family run a **grocery shop** in Phnom Penh, Cambodia.

Narinder and his wife run a grocery shop in Oxford, in the United Kingdom (UK).

Gloria and her family have a grocery shop in Cayambe, Ecuador.

Selling you food

Food shops are different in different countries. They are even different in the same country.

Bob's **supermarket** is on the edge of town. He does not live there. It is a 10 minutes' drive to work from his home.

Sovon and her family live above the shop. It is very hot in Cambodia. People spend lots of time outside. Their home can be very noisy.

Narinder's family also live above their shop. They live on a busy road, like Sovon's family. But there is not as much noise from the street.

Gloria's family live behind the shop. You can just see the white wall of their yard. The shop is on the main road into town.

USA

Bob Tait's **supermarket** sells **groceries**, drinks, sweets and cakes, fresh fruit and vegetables, bread, frozen food, ice and even flowers and plants. Most of the people who use Bob's shop are **local** people, but they still drive there. They often shop for a week or two, and buy too much to carry home on foot.

Here Bob is helping a **customer** choose between all the different sorts of orange juice he sells.

The supermarket is open for 24 hours every day. Bob does not work all the time. He has lots of people working for him. He can choose when to go to work.

Bob's **suppliers** often have new things for him to try. Here he and his wife, Joan, are talking about a new kind of **detergent**.

The Taits cannot just buy a few bottles to try in the shop. Their suppliers want them to buy a lot at a time. So they have to think hard before they buy new things. Will their **customers** want to buy them?

Bob, Joan and their children, Bobby and Andy, eat their main meal together in the evening. The boys are out at school all day. They eat as soon as Bob gets in from work, about 6 pm. Here they are eating beef and vegetable stew, salad and hot bread rolls. They are drinking milk.

Cambodia

Yim Sovon and her family sell **groceries**, medicines, sweets, cakes, drinks, and almost anything else she thinks **local** people will need.

Sovon does not buy a lot at a time, because the shop is small and there is not a lot of space to **store** things.

Here a boy has come to buy some cooking oil. Sovon is measuring it out for him.

Sovon's **customers** do not often buy a lot of things all at once. Most people shop for what they need each day. A lot of the things Sovon sells come to her in big sacks or tins. Sovon then sells each person just as much as they need.

The shop opens every day, for most of the day. Sovon's husband, Thorn, is a policeman. He has no time to help in the shop. Sovon's mother helps, and so do her two children, when they are not in school. Here Sovon's daughter, Sarun, is serving a **customer**.

Sovon's family eat their main meal together in the middle of the day. They eat their meal in a room at the back of the shop. Here they are eating rice, vegetables and fish.

United Kingdom

Narinder Singh Bhella sells **groceries**, fresh vegetables and fruit, sweets, bread and drinks. His shop is quite a big shop. It has lots of different things for **customers** to choose from.

Narinder's customers are mostly **local** people. His shop is in the middle of lots of streets of houses. People can easily walk there. They often come in every few days.

The shop is open from 8 am to 8 pm every day apart from Sunday, when it closes at 5 pm.

Narinder and his wife, Parvesh, do most of the work in the shop. They have one helper who comes in nearly every day. The children are too young to help a lot. They go to nursery school three days a week. Here Parvesh is putting prices on some food.

The family eat their main meal together
in the middle of the day, when the children
get home from nursery school. The shop
is shut while they eat their lunch.

Here they are eating savoury rice,
yoghurt and salad. They are drinking
orange juice.

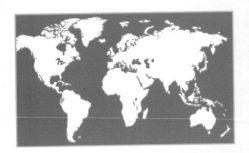

Ecuador

Gloria Hernandez's shop sells **groceries**, drinks, bread and some fresh fruit and vegetables. She also sells sweets and ice cream.

There is a telephone in the shop that **customers** can use, and tables for them to sit and drink or chat at. Most of Gloria's customers are **local** people.

A lot of customers do not come into the shop and sit down. They stand at the door like these boys, and tell Gloria what they want to buy. Gloria then fetches it for them.

The shop is open every day. It is open from 6 am to 10.30 pm. Sometimes it stays open even later. It only closes on important holidays, like Christmas Day.

Gloria's children go to school all
morning, from 7.30 am to 1 pm.
Gloria has a helper in the shop until
they get back, then they help.

Here Gloria's **nephew**, Patrizo, is
answering the phone. Her daughters,
Elizabeth and Monica, will help in the
shop once they have done their
homework.

The family eat their main meal in the middle of the day, in the kitchen behind the shop. They do not all eat together, because the shop does not shut for lunch. They are eating meat and vegetable stew and bread.

Factfile

Cambodia

Population: 9 million

Capital city: Phnom Penh

United Kingdom (UK)

Population: 58 million

Capital city: London

Ecuador

Population: 11 million

Capital city: Quito

United States of America (USA)

Population: 264 million

Capital city: Washington DC

Digging deeper

1 Look at page 3. What different ways of travelling can you see?

2 Look at page 4. What do you think the weather is like in Iowa, USA and in Cambodia? Why do you think this?

3 Look at pages 14 and 18. How are the shops in the UK and Ecuador the same? How are they different?

Glossary

customer a person who comes to a shop (or other business) to buy something

detergent something that is used to clean things. Detergents can come as a liquid or powder. Washing-up liquid, washing powder, dishwasher powder and floor cleaner are all detergents.

groceries dried foods like flour, sugar, rice, tea, and dried and tinned fruit, vegetable and beans

grocery shop a shop that sells groceries. These shops usually sell other things too, like cleaning things for the house, toilet paper, soap, shampoo and matches.

local coming from the same area. In a village everyone in the village would be called a local person. Big towns or cities often have lots of smaller areas, each with local names and local shops.

nephew the son of your brother or sister is your nephew

store when you store something you put it away to use or sell later on

supermarket a large shop that sells food and lots of other things. In supermarkets you collect all the things you want to buy and pay for them just before you leave the shop.

suppliers people who sell shops the things they need

Index

First published in Great Britain by Heinemann Library
Halley Court, Jordan Hill, Oxford OX2 8EJ
a division of Reed Educational and Professional Publishing Ltd

OXFORD FLORENCE PRAGUE MADRID ATHENS MELBOURNE
AUCKLAND KUALA LUMPUR SINGAPORE TOKYO IBADAN
NAIROBI KAMPALA JOHANNESBURG GABORONE PORTSMOUTH
NH CHICAGO MEXICO CITY SAO PAULO

© Reed Educational and Professional Publishing Ltd 1996

Designed by John Walker

Illustrations by Oxford Illustrators and Visual Image

Printed in Malaysia

00 99 98 97 96

10 9 8 7 6 5 4 3 2 1

ISBN 0 431 06338 9

British Library Cataloguing in Publication Data
Hudson, Margaret
Shopkeeper
I. Merchants – Juvenile literature
I. Title
381.1'092

Acknowledgements

The Publishers would like to thank the following for permission to reproduce photographs.

Chris Honeywell: pp. 1, 3, 4, 14-17;

Martin Flitman/Oxfam: pp. 3, 4, 10-13;

Rhodri Jones/Oxfam: pp. 3, 5, 18-21;

Steve Benbow: pp. 3, 5, 6-9

Cover photograph reproduced with permission of Martin Flitman.

Our thanks to Clare Boast for her comments in the preparation of this book.

Every effort has been made to contact copyright holders of any material reproduced in this book. Any omissions will be rectified in subsequent printings if notice is given to the Publisher.

Oxfam believes that all people have basic rights: to earn a living, to have food, shelter, health care and education. There are nine Oxfam organizations around the world - they work with poor people in over 70 countries. Oxfam provides relief in emergencies, and gives long term support to people who are working to make life better for themselves and their families.

Oxfam (UK and Ireland) produces a catalogue of resources for schools and young people. For a copy contact Oxfam, 274 Banbury Road, Oxford, OX2 7DZ (tel. 01865 311311) or contact your national Oxfam office.

Oxfam UK and Ireland is a Registered Charity number 202918.
Oxfam UK and Ireland is a member of Oxfam International.